GW00502124

I shall be very
busy polishing,
this day. I may
forget Thee, but do
not Thou forget me
/Amen

1

HANDLE WITH PRAYER

A Church Cleaner's Notebook

by Graham Jeffery

Published for the Council for the Care of Churches

CHURCH HOUSE PUBLISHING
Church House, Great Smith Street, London SW1P 3NZ

ISBN 0 7151 7562 9

Published 1992 for the Council for the Care of Churches by Church House Publishing

Printed in England by Rapier Press

based on an idea

by Henry Stapleton

Dear Lord,
    You knit together
    so many people
    in one communion and fellowship;
    grant that we
           who stitch and sew, polish and prepare
           may also, by your grace,
           unify the true temple,
               that company of all believers,
                  to the glory of
                      Your name

St Martha the
Martyr to household
Chores —

Matins 11 am

Cleaning a church, as indeed any home, is a very spiritual business. You do not need a book to tell you that. 'Who sweeps a room, as for God's laws, makes that and the action fine.' No doubt all water is holy water, all wine sacramental, not just that in the vestry cupboard. When this is said though, there remains a special place for those who care for their local church. Whether this be early Saxon or Victorian, it is a visible expression of Christianity: a place where God's voice is heard, not just in sermon or reading, but in pew and kneeler; and in the general appearance of things.

What follows then is a sort of 'manual', and we hope encouragement, for that unseen band of helpers who labour to keep the churches of our land 'open all hours'. And to make of them, a second 'home' for our people. Please God, through their labours and yours, the voice of Jesus himself will be heard again: 'Come to me all who travail and are heavy laden, and I will refresh you'.

9

The Noticeboard

Probably the first thing people see.
It may not bring people into church
but that is no reason to keep them out.
Neatly painted
Time of services clear.
Rector or wardens' names or phone numbers,
                              if appropriate.
Needs to be repainted, probably
every seven or eight years.
Wash very gently
to clean. The
paint will almost
certainly peel.

The Porch

Is the doorway to God's house.
It needs to be welcoming and tidy.
One or two kind notices: not too many.
Are old ones taken away?
There is a place for some old ones, for
interest's sake. But out-of-date notices
are best out of sight.

Ask sometimes: does this notice need to be there?
The congregation and visitors need to be stimulated by new things
attractively printed.

It is not an advertising agency.

The Desk Inside

The West End can be as important as the east end.

Visitors come to see the church, or worship,
Not to see piles of old literature.
Too many appeals simply 'blur' the mind.
The church is the best advertisement for itself.
Visitors' book.
Cards. Need to be tidied daily.

A few books carefully chosen, can be helpful and appropriate.

Copies of the Four Gospels are probably best.

The Wall Safe

Needs to be clear.
A note of thanks.
This can be a source
of income to the church,
and even if it is not,
it is nice to say thank you.

The Font

The place where most of us begin our journey,
in one way
or another.
True doorway to church.
Should be blessed,
noted and highlighted.

The Floors

The part most used by everyone,
and only noticed if muddy,
not otherwise. Quite unfair on the
cleaners, this. But quite inevitable.

1. Please keep floors clear of dust
2. Hoover carpets regularly
3. Beware accumulation of dirt under straw matting
4. Wash stone floors sparingly
5. If previously polished, polish wooden floors and tiles.

O all ye holy dusters
and needlewomen,
bless ye the Lord
praise him and
magnify him forever

The Walls

At least people do not walk on the walls, though the church cleaner can well be driven *up* them. Brush with a light feather brush. Remember, for all their cracks and blemishes, like you they help to keep the church up.

Bless This Heater

Low HIGH Infernal

The Windows

Are most clearly seen inside,
least clearly outside.
They are or used to be
the sermon of the common man.

Plain glass shows the dirt
more easily, but can give
a good view of the world
which awaits us after the blessing.

No vim, abrasives, or additives, please.
The stained glass details may disappear!

Brasses

Do not polish mediaeval brass.
More recent brass can be polished,
but beware of leaving polish on surrounding walls.

Memorials

St Tishoo the
Ticklish 1319-98

Keep well dusted.
Take advice about cleaning marbles.
Consult your architect.

Saint Rottweiler
the ninth. 1403-69

Those who stitch and sew,
	also prepare.
Those who polish and dust,
	also assist.
Those who sweep the pulpit steps,
	though never entering it
	help to proclaim
	this is the Lord's house
	and he loves us all.

The Pulpit

The rector may not always preach from the pulpit nowadays, and obviously whatever is said here matters *more* than the way it is polished. Even so, the pulpit is a focal point of all churches: and in some churches, a valuable one. Also, feeding the woodwork, as indeed the congregation, is more important than a quick 'shine'. Please check the reading desk; any curtains or 'surrounds', and . . . the floorboards!

34

The Pews

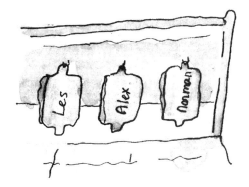

The place where most of the congregation
spend most of their time. Therefore
the place where most work is done:
or prayed for, or thought of. The place where
souls are blessed, and the kingdom realized.

Is there somewhere to hang the hassocks?
Do they need it?
(Does it matter?)

The Altar

Are the flowers fresh?
One bowl or spray of fresh flowers
is worth twenty whose leaves are drooping.

The East End may be the poorer part of some
cities, but it is the richest part of this
one. Not visited much, except once a week:
but viewed all the time. Though the sanctuary
points beyond itself to God, nice hangings and
beautiful flowers can help the soul on
its way.

38

The Vestry

The most functional room of all.
Scarcely seen by the congregation,
and only by the bride and groom
when they sign the registers.

Again, needs to be tidy.
Place for robes clearly defined.
Service book and pen on the table.
The fewer things about, the better.
Tidiness may not be next to godliness
in the next life, but here on earth
the rector wants to be able to find
his sermon notes.

Store the bread and wine carefully,
and the candles separately.

The Organ

Needs its own special care and servicing,
and there is probably little the poor cleaner
can do about it . . .
except remember, dust is a
great enemy of organs. And by
your care of the church generally,
you help the bride come in to her
favourite 'March' on Saturday afternoon.

The Hymn Board

Here again, the church needs
to look as though it is used.
Next Sunday's hymns on the
board may not be possible,
but last Sunday's should
(probably) be taken down.

The Churchyard

Deserves and has a book to itself (*The Churchyards Handbook*).
There is no need for everything to be mown flat.
The only place where some wild flowers can grow.
Old gravestones can only be cared for as appropriate (and possible).

Hedges should possibly be low for reasons of security.
Is the gate properly kept, and the pathway clear?
Is the church locked at night?
Old flowers should be taken away.
A place for them in some appropriate corner.
A garden of remembrance?
Not too many memorials.
A wooden seat (fixed) to sit on and rest
is better than a lot of 'tablets'.

Try cutting the grass at different lengths.
Keep part of the churchyard
as a conservation area.

The churchyard can also be a place of prayer
wherein God's servants meet.

Outhouses

Need to be tidy, within view,
and probably locked. Petrol for
the mower and other things
should be carefully stored away.

We need to set our souls on fire,
but not much else.

I have been very busy this day. I may have forgotten Thee. Thank-you for not forgetting me

And I will dwell in the
house of the Lord forever.

Psalm 23.